Life

Life

DONNA
ASHWORTH

BLACK & WHITE PUBLISHING

First published in the UK in 2022 by
Black & White Publishing Ltd
Nautical House, 104 Commercial Street, Edinburgh, EH6 6NF

A division of Bonnier Books UK
4th Floor, Victoria House, Bloomsbury Square, London, WC1B 4DA
Owned by Bonnier Books
Sveavägen 56, Stockholm, Sweden

A CIP catalogue record for this book is available from the British Library.

ISBN: 978 1 78530 444 6

5 7 9 10 8 6 4

Typeset by Iolaire Typesetting, Newtonmore
Printed and bound in Great Britain by Clays Ltd, Elcograf S.p.A.

www.blackandwhitepublishing.com

To the people I have learned from along the way, I dedicate this book to you. Thank you for taking time to share your lessons with me, and to guide me when I wavered. Because of you, I shall go on to do the same. And where sharing exists, peace grows and joy thrives.

AUTHOR'S NOTE

Ah but what is life if not *everything*. All the ups, *all* the downs, all the ins and outs, sometimes over and over in the same day. It is a ride, no question, and a bumpy one at that. But if you are seeking joy, looking for beauty and deciding to choose love every day, it can be such a joyous ride my friend. I hope this book will help with that. And sometimes, I hope it will just remind you that you are not alone, never alone.

CONTENTS

ah but what is life if not

everything

sometimes all in the flicker of a
moment

LIFE

Life is short, they say
and it's for the living, they add
but they don't tell you how hard it is
how much pain it can bring
and how some of us
though gifted time
cannot make it to the end.

I have found that life is everything
sometimes in one day
it is exhilarating
terrifying
joyful
heartbreaking.

And whilst it is true that *life is not fair*
I believe we all get our share
of the good, the bad and the ugly.

And the secret of life, I think
is to roll
to bend
to yield
to adapt to the new
and let the old go
when it is time.

I think, the secret of life
is to laugh when you must
and cry when you should
and let everything else come and go.

Except love
that must always stay
that's the only way.

YOUR PERFECT

If you are not broken
bruised
weathered
and worn
where have you been my friend?

If your battered heart
does not still break
every day
then perhaps
you are not paying attention?

Don't aim to come out of this life
preserved and perfect
you're supposed to crumble
and rebuild
a million times over
until your soul is satisfied
you have given your all.

Because that's why you are here.

Your perfect is not needed
but your broken
is very important

very important
indeed.

WEEKEND

Forget about all the things you didn't do over the weekend. Forget also about all the things you did do, that you now wish you hadn't. Life is not for suffering, you are *supposed* to feel joyous, to feel free, to feel alive sometimes. So if you have felt any of those things recently, even for a moment, be *proud*. That's what you're here for. And sometimes, stepping off the treadmill (or even falling), is the best thing we can do. Forget about all the things you didn't get right this weekend and instead pat yourself on the back for remembering that life is for the living.

THE INTERRUPT

I'm sorry if I interrupt you
I'm completely invested you see.

I'm so very much invested
in everything you're saying
that my brain is firing
firing *spectacularly*
on all the similarities
and fusions
between what you are saying
and what I am feeling
and I *know*
that these thoughts
will not stay there for long
so if I blurt out
if I interrupt
it's because
you have really sparked a connection.

It's not rudeness
though it may seem so
it's absolute utter
appreciation.

It's one happy brain syncing
quite beautifully
with another.

THIS IS NO WAITING ROOM

What if you didn't wake up tomorrow
and your soul is watching down
thinking of all the things you didn't get to do yet
because you were too scared
or too shy
or too worried about money.

And all the things you told yourself
you weren't good enough for
swam in front of your eyes
fighting for a place in the line
beside the words you didn't say
and the joy you forgot to have.

My friend, there is absolutely no room
for anything in your day
other than *acceptance*
you will never have enough money, or time
and you will certainly never have that perfect body
the world told you to want to be happy.

And before you say it's too late
to embrace this thing we call life
no it is not
you can do it right where you are
right this minute
get outside, breathe, look at the trees
put your bare feet on the grass
hand on your heart to feel that pulse
and that's it.

You're living.

Keep that up.

Wait up for the moon sometimes
or get up early to see a sunrise
just because you can
jump in the lake
run, skip, dance
the things you need to feel alive
are all around
you just have to see them.

Let in opportunity
and say yes to the invitations that scare you a little
in a good way.

Say no to some of the things you force yourself to do
knowing they rinse you of your peace.

Life was never supposed to be a waiting room
it was supposed to be a hillside
with paths leading in every direction
and mountains as far as the eye can see
hiding adventures and new friends behind them.

Don't let yourself get to the end of this ride
without having stopped to smell those beautiful roses
that's the only thing you need to fear in this life
everything else is all part of it.

It's all just a messy, complicated, beautiful
and terrifying part of it.

Chin up, throw your arms wide open
and let it be so.

SAY IT

Never be afraid
to let someone know
if they brightened the room
they just walked into.

Or if something they said
inspired you to change.

Never be embarrassed
to share a compliment with a stranger
and don't ever fall into the trap of believing
that the people you love *know* that.

Say it.

Always say it.

Your words may land a little awkwardly at first
but in the dark of the night
those seeds will plant themselves
into someone's mental garden
and start to germinate
gather strength and bloom.

Sow seeds
wherever you go.

There is nothing better you can do with your words

than plant a precious seed.

WOMEN

In this life we women are many things
mothers, sisters, wives, friends, carers.

We are creators
we are nurture
we are *home*.

But above all
we women are the magic
we are the intuition.

We are the product of generations
who fought to be heard
to be believed
to be empowered.

And that runs very deep.

When women come together
magic happens my friend.

And those who tell you otherwise are afraid.

We are not.

So come together in all your glory when you can
because you can
because you *must*
because you are called by deep-seated ancestry to do so.

And because, most of all
we hold up half the sky
and our half must show the other

how to be.

ONE

If you wonder why you wane with the moon and take power from the sun, it is because you are one. The oceans, too, call you for a reason. You are made of everything they are, and they are made of you. Atoms, compounds and stardust, all of us. We all came from the same and we all end the same. So if you feel pulled by nature, pulled by the forces that suspend our planet in its place. It's because you are, my friend. *You are*.

MOTHER NATURE WANTS A WORD

She wants to remind you
how over-stretched you are
how exhausted you are
how much you need a rest.

She knows you see that
and she wants you to keep it close
now life is getting busy again.

No more using stress, tiredness
and lack of time
as badges of honour
you know that life doesn't have to be a race
you know what value lies
in the silence and the peace
you met yourself again
and she wants you to hold on tight.

Most of all she wants you to remember
that the world won't stop if you do.

Only Mother Nature can stop the world.

Take it slowly child of the universe
you're not here to burn out
you're here to burn brightly.

Protect that precious light of yours
you only get one.

POINTLESS

I know it seems pointless
to perform the day-to-day
sometimes
when there is so much suffering
elsewhere.

But don't forget that your pointless
your nitty-gritty
your mundane
is someone else's paradise.

And that this world will always be full
of someone experiencing every colour
of the spectrum
at all times.

When the day-to-day feels pointless
in the face of others' suffering
remember
that your *pointless*
is someone else's *paradise*
so give it your all.

Because you *can*
for them.

And you must.
for *you*.

TO THE WOMAN WHO HAS TAKEN TOO MUCH

To the woman who has given too much
to the woman who has no idea
how she will keep going like this
every day.

I see you.

I see how exhausted you are.
I see your desire to run for the hills
without a care in the world.

And I know that if you did so
the world which you have created
would collapse
without you
so, of course
that is not an option.

And I know
just how oppressive the weight of that can be
how suffocating it is
how scary that feels sometimes.

And I also know
how *grateful* you are for this load you carry
for it's everything you need
and yet all that consumes you.

And that's okay.

It is okay to feel weary
even when the weight is that of your *blessings*
it is still heavy to carry.

There is no space for shame
in that load of yours
no space for guilt
no space for perfection
set those down.

Lighten your load of those things.

Next, take out the need
to conform to others' expectations
and gather up all the past mistakes
and the worries for the future.

They can all go.

Lastly, the spaces you have just made
should be filled with rest
for we know that resting is very much doing
and then add in your joy.
And whatever space is left
leave it there.

Ready for new things
things which will show up
as soon as they see their space waiting.

It's high time they did.

CAGE

Sometimes things crumble around you not because you are losing everything but because the life you built has become your cage and you don't need a cage my friend, you don't need a cage. You need fresh, open spaces with room to breathe, room to roam, room to reach out and room to grow. Sometimes things crumble around you, simply because you built them too well. Let it crumble. It no longer serves you and it's high time you broke out.

AND YOU CAN

You may not know
exactly where you're going
in this life
but you know
you're not going backwards.

You may not know
where you will end up
but something deep inside
tells you
it will be exactly where
you're supposed to be.

You can't be sure
what's in store for you
on this journey
but you can decide
that you won't be broken
in the same way twice.

You see, you've learned from your mistakes
you've grown through your struggles
you've weathered every storm sent to test you.

And yes there will be troubles anew
there will be untold twists
in your story yet to come.

But nothing negative need be repeated
not if you can help it my friend.

And you can.

NUMB

Right now you're living in survival mode
you're numb, lifeless, exhausted
now and again you feel that panic
when you realise how far you've sailed
from your old self

but this is temporary.

You're doing what your human instinct
told you to do.

You're hunkered down
getting through, *enduring*

it's not permanent.

When your world feels safe again
when you take the first tentative steps
back out there
you'll resurface
your spark will reignite
lightly at first
but then brighter than ever before.

Right now
you're living in survival mode
and that's ok my friend.

You'll be back.

You never really left.

THE BEST ADVICE

It really doesn't matter how clean you eat
how fit you are
and how many sacrifices you make
for your health.

Aside from a few very bad things you can do
like extremes of anything
you will live as long and as healthily
as *you will live*.

It's luck, it's genes
it's actually a complete mystery.

Doctors die from cancer too
athletes drop dead just like that
some people who drink die young
and some people who don't, do too.

Perfect people
at the perfect, ultimate prime of their life
are taken every day.
Just like that.

It's a lottery and no one can call it.
We all have a story of someone who did everything right
yet couldn't keep their place here on this earth.

I'm not saying do not care for your body
of course not
but the best advice I have come across my friends
is to *live*.

To laugh
smile

sing
walk
swim
breathe
rest
meditate
enjoy
share
listen
love
kiss
run
giggle
misbehave
taste, really taste
all of these things will do your body
your mind
and your soul
so much good.

To refuse to swallow bitterness
anger
regret
jealousy
and fear
for they are the poisons

we should really watch out for.

YOUR SHOULDERS

Your shoulders are tired
your shoulders are weary
who said you must carry all that?

You didn't sign up for it
you didn't volunteer to be the bearer
but still you've come to bear it
and you cannot find a place
to lay it down.

Your shoulders are tired
lift them up
let them down
roll them around
release.

Now shake your head
from side to side
and say *no*
sometimes
just sometimes.

Because it's the saying no
the letting *go*
that your shoulders
really need.

A LOT

I could tell you
to make amazing things happen
today
this week
this year.

And maybe you would.

But what I really want to tell you
is how amazing
what you already do every day is.

It's a lot my friend

your life is a *lot*
the world is a *lot*
your mind is a *lot*.

So today
this week
this year
why don't you take some time
to look at what you already do
and what an impressive machine
you actually are.

You're a whole lot
(and that's more than enough).

REST

If only we could see the power in rest. If only we could attach to it the worth it so deserves. If only we could open our minds to the idea that everything in nature has its time to rise and its time to descend. That each of these acts is as important as the other. And that is exactly as it must be. If only the ability to allow our bodies space to heal was awarded the same badge of honour given to busyness and stress in this life. If only we could realise, resting is very much *doing*.

THE COST

The *fitting in* has cost me
it's cost me dear indeed
I took off parts that were too much
in order to succeed

I wrestled with my largeness
I did my best to shrink
I tried to round my edges
to filter what I think

I shaved off all my quirks
and I learned to bite my tongue
I locked my heart up with a key
I did that very young

The fitting in has cost me
it's cost me dear indeed
why learn to fit their pattern
when you're born to take the lead.

WAR AND HOPE

On every day the sun rises
there is war somewhere
and there has always *been*
war somewhere.

But on every day the sun rises
there is peace somewhere too.

And the people in the peaceful places
wish with all their heart
that they could share their peace
but all they can do is share a little money
or prayers
or a bed
so they *do*.

And they hope
most importantly they *hope*.

Because it's that *hope*
in its mass
which matters.

That *hope*
in such numbers
and the kindness
from the peaceful
is what keeps the balance from tipping.

And it's *vital* to keep that balance from tipping.

So stay hopeful my friend
stay kind, stay peaceful.

You're already playing your part
just by being you.

DON'T MISS YOUR OWN PARTY

When you prepare for days to ensure a gathering
is the most perfect it can possibly be.

But you miss the whole thing
because you are so very busy
doing and not being.

Don't let that be the metaphor for your life.

Don't let the moment you finally relax
be a moment too far.

I guess what I am trying to say is
don't miss your own party
because you wanted everyone else
to have the best time.

Now is the time to sit down
take a beat and chat with a friend
or loved one
now is the time to eat
break bread and be merry
now is the time to be fully here
fully present, enjoying, experiencing
living.

Not after
not when everything is *perfect.*

The dishes can wait
this is your party
your life
you're invited too.

LESS

To the woman
who may somehow feel less today
because she dropped a ball
missed a deadline
forgot something *important*
or failed to be all things to all people
in the most perfect of ways

you are not alone.

Everyone else felt that way today too
it's as common as a nose on a face
and it should cause you no shame
worry or regret.

You will most likely
get things wrong again tomorrow
such is life.

No one gets it just right
how could they
when it is not possible.

You are a flawed
ball-dropping
wonderful human being
with a million intricate patterns
faults, flaws and foibles
intertwined so complexly
in your beautiful kaleidoscope soul.

And so am I.

How wonderful.

LET HER OUT

I can tell you why you cannot seem
to become that woman
you so very much aspire to be
she is not you.

You are, quite wrongly
chasing an ideal of a woman
you will never be.

And you are
quite wrongly
ignoring the woman
you already so very much are.

And peace will not come
until you take a deep hard look at yourself
and see the plethora of wonder
grace and humanity
all wrapped up, a little messily
into a loveable parcel of realness.

Humans do not come perfectly packaged
with a warranty or guarantee.

We are miracles of science, nature and a little magic.

Born of centuries of incredible ancestors
who walked through fire and ice
to bring us to life.

And we cannot be tamed into a neat little box.

Stop chasing the ideal of a woman
you were not born to be
and start embracing she
who is fizzing fiercely to be seen
right in front of your eyes.

Let her out.

if you are not yet broken and rebuilt

many times over

where have you been my friend?

SLEEP WON'T HELP

If it's your soul which is exhausted.

Food won't satisfy a hunger
for acceptance, love or adventure.

An empty void can't be filled
with material possessions or holidays.

A bountiful bank account won't buy
health or happiness.

If you aren't watering the seeds of your joy
your life will never flower
and no amount of expensive decoration
will make it blossom.

Sleep won't help
if it's your soul which is exhausted
but the good news is
the remedies you need
are free and plentiful
and they are all around you
hiding in plain sight
amongst the everyday.

BE THE PEACE

When it seems we are being dragged
from one traumatic period
straight into another
remember
we know what to do.

We keep the fear at arm's length
because we know that letting it in
past its rightful place is debilitating.

We keep the hope high
and the kindness higher
and we go about our daily lives
in the simplest most basic of ways
being grateful for what matters
and letting happiness in when it shows up.

There is little we can do to control the world
but we can control our reaction to it
and we can remember
that everything is temporary
and anything can change in a heartbeat.

So if peace is your aim
then be the peace you seek.

When there is no peace to be found
you can bring it
you can *be* it.

UNSTOPPABLE

Unstoppable they called her
but I saw her stop
I saw her stop
many many times.

Sometimes
I thought she had stopped
for good

but no
she always found a way
to resurrect.

To rise again.

Not the same
never the same.

Each time a little more determined
and a little less vulnerable.

Unstoppable they said
but I think
it was in the stopping

that she found
her power.

CIRCUS

Sometimes, you have to drop a few plates
watch them smash on the ground
and shout, this is my circus
I'm tired of being a clown

I'm the ringmaster now
and I decide who stays
I decide who sits to watch
I decide who pays

This tightrope, it's far too high
and far too bloody thin
these animals are tired of crowds
of being trapped within

I'm cutting it down
and setting them loose
I'm tired of living this folly
this smile is painted on my face
the mask of eternal jolly

I'm closing the tent
I'm done with the show
it's time to shut this down
if you've come to see a spectacle
then please do turn around

There's nothing to see here
nothing to watch
today I'm breaking free
time for me to have all the fun
time for me to flee

Sometimes you have to drop a few plates
let them smash on the ground
the crash of your containment
can be a wonderful sound.

CRASHED

She crashed, rather spectacularly, on the craggy peaks of rock bottom. To say that she shattered into a thousand pieces would not be doing it justice. So, if you find that she no longer cares for your judgement, or your suffocating expectations. If she seems oblivious to your dramas and your chaos. Perhaps it's because she left those jagged little pieces out when she rebuilt herself again. She crashed, yes she did, but if you think her easy to *break*, think again.

DECIDE

Just decide
to love the heck out of your life
and if you truly *can't*
then you simply must
make it more loveable.

Change things around.

Move things out
add things in.

It's your life
you can do that.

If you really truly cannot change things around
change the way you *see* things
change your *view* on the things in your life.

Do whatever you need to do
to get any kind of joy
every day.

And start now
right this minute.

The future is promised to no one
what are you waiting for?

This is it my friend
this is it.

YOUR BEST DAYS

By all means rest
and go low when you must
lay on the bottom
and allow the darkness to consume you
sometimes, that's the only way.

But when the light starts to stroke your eyelids
just a tiny glimmer
and you feel a faint bubble of hope
sparking into life
somewhere deep within your gut
wake up my friend
for the love of all that is good
let that bubble fizz and pop
and create more bubbles
and use them to prize open your eyes
and restart your weary heart.

Because some of your best days
some of your *finest* moments
where the sun warms every bone
in your broken body
and life feels like a beautiful dream

have not even happened yet.

Some of your most wonderful memories
are waiting to be made

you need to show up for that.

SPARK

We are born, each of us, with a unique flash of brilliance. A spark so distracting, that this militant world tries desperately hard to thrash it out of us, for how could a world so full of intricately fabulous individuals be easily controlled? So, if you kept hold of that thing my friend, or found it again in the wilderness of this life, resurrecting it bravely despite the resistance, well done to you. Keep holding on tight to that magnificence. That's yours. That is *all yours*.

SUMMER BODY

Summer is going to have to make do
with my winter body again this year.

Unchanged.

Except perhaps a little lighter
oh not from less food
and more exercise
no, not that.

From releasing the weight
of society's expectation
of how I should look in a swimsuit

detoxing my brain of the conditioning
drummed into us from childhood.

I've much better things to do
than look great for the eyes of strangers
on a beach somewhere.

I have magic to make, stories to weave
and adventures to begin.

I have food to taste
wonders to see
and seas in which I must swim.

Summer is going to have to make do
with my winter body again this year.

No apologies from me.

YOUR WORTH IS YOUR CASTLE

Your worth's entirely precious
give the build your all
let the walls be strong
let the gates be tall
let the bricks withstand
any change of plan
any comment, any sneaky twist
of life's right hand

Let your moat be full
bring your drawbridge up
when the numbers rise
when the times get tough
you're not something to be packaged
you're not measured by your width
you're a human made of love, of light
of the wishes that you wish

Get your highs from feeling strong
when the buttons just won't meet
let the lows attack the brick
but don't let them through the keep
if your body weight decides
how you go about your life
retreat within your walls
this is not your fight

No-one ever talked of death
and wished they'd been more slim
no-one ever looked behind
and wished those demons in.

PASSING ON

Passing on clothes
which no longer fit you
is not a failure my friend
quite the opposite.

It is empowering.

Breaking free.

It is respecting
and honouring change.

We are all changing
sometimes one way
sometimes another
and that's not only okay
it is *necessary.*

Staying the same
is not what you are here for.

You are here to grow.

Passing on things
which no longer serve you
is not a failure my friend
quite the opposite.

MIRROR

Mirror mirror on the wall
I see no care if I'm big or small
you see I realised long ago
that looking at you brings such woe
and so instead I looked within
and made a pact that I'd begin
to see myself clear in my head
and take away the mirror dread
so now when I catch my reflection
I do not notice my complexion
instead I see a friend I know
someone I like from head to toe
and if perhaps you feel the same
allow these words to break that chain
the mirror should not be your foe
it's time to let that struggle go
mirror mirror on the wall
I shall not catch you when you fall
because my worth is not in you
it's somewhere safe
attached like glue.

WHEN YOU CANNOT BEAR YOUR BODY

The days when you cannot bear to exist
within your own body
are the days you must really sit there
and feel the vessel you live in.

Consider its structure
the layers, the insides
the many miraculous functions
in every single moment.

If it lives with disability
consider the pressure that brings
to each and every sinew.

If it is fighting illness
imagine that war within you daily
and the battles won and lost.

Stare at your body
absorb it, touch it
let the feelings of shame and disgust
engulf you
and then send them away to the universe
to be disposed of.

You are not your body
you are a guest in your body
and you are currently rejecting it daily.

This rejection creates dysfunction
and estrangement
it is little wonder you feel uncomfortable
within your own skin
you are.

You, my friend
did not ruin your body
or let yourself go
you are merely living
and life takes its toll
as it absolutely must.

The days when you cannot bear
to exist within your body
are the days when your body needs you
so very much
to check in
to accept
to apologise
to connect
to befriend.

Be grateful
as every guest should be.

Be tidy
be respectful
be kind.

But most of all
be good company.

You are not here for long.

I HAVE BEEN HER

I have been her
I have been she
I have been them
and now I'm me

I have been out
and I've been in
I've felt defeat
I've known the win

I have held joy
and shouldered grief
I've had my share
of changed beliefs

I have been hurt
and I've been high
I found no answers
to what and why

I know the loss
and I know the gain
I know that we
all bleed the same

I have been her
I have been she
I have been them
and now I'm *me*.

WHAT IS WISDOM

What is wisdom
if not the realisation
that none of it matters
that the only things to ever matter
were the first things to be sacrificed
whilst chasing a *life*.

What is wisdom
if not the knowing
that we are here for one thing
and for one thing only
to *love*
and that you cannot find love
in a new house, a fast car
or a glittering career.

What is wisdom
if not finally accepting
that you are who you are
and that everyone else is who they are
and that the world is what it is
and that is that.

What is wisdom
if not peace
after a battle
that was never yours to fight
a war that was never yours to win
and a life that was far too full of drama
stress and suffering.

What is wisdom
if not forgiveness
and finally
the letting go.

MOUNTAINS

Oh but you must look behind you or you may not recall the mountains. The ones you thought you'd die on. The ones you scaled and survived with such bravery and passion. And then you'll look at the mountain ahead of you and realise you've done it before. You've done much harder before, in fact. And you'll do it *again*. Oh but you must look behind you sometimes my love, even if just to see, how very much you are.

FUEL

The fuel for your fire is homemade:

a self-accepting thought
a peaceful afternoon
a good deed done
a beloved memory shared
a song that sparks your heart
a treat for your soul
a rest for your weary bones
a break from criticism
a moment spent in love.

All of these things
stoke the flames
that drive you on.

Keep that fire burning brightly.

You may not even know this
but your light
leads the way
for so many.

YOUR TO-DO LIST

Your to-do list can wait
it is later than you think
and you cannot ask for time back
once it's gone

At work you'll be replaced
but at home you just cannot
and your presence is the one thing
they most want

There are bills that must be paid
but at the end of all your days
it's the love you shared that keeps
your people fed

They can forge a better life
knowing you were by their side
and the stories that you made
will be their bread

Your to-do list can wait
it is later than you think
and you cannot ask for time back
when it's passed

You're not here to break your back
doing every little task
you are here to make the memories
that will last.

THE TRICK

The trick is to live a life you won't be sad about, if your time is up too soon. And it won't be the houses, the cars or the accolades you count, should that untimely moment arise. It will be the love. Even if that love was solely for yourself, in the end, as long as you did it with passion. Whatever you do, whomever you love, do it with **passion**. Because it is that which your soul will take with it, on its journey to who knows where.

STOP

The world won't stop still if you do
the tides will not cease to flow
the sun will still rise and set if
you take some time out alone

The sky will still rumble if you rest
the days will still move into night
the world will continue to turn if
your fire needs time to ignite

The people will breathe still without you
the chores will stay patiently there
the things on your list will not wander
if you take time out for self-care

The world won't stop still if you do
so fear not the tears in your eyes
they wash and they clear up your vision
and that's how you reset and rise.

SAND

We are always running out of time
and we know it.

So we move *faster*
do *more*
fill life to the full
to make it count.

When what we really should be doing
is *slowing* down
stopping
taking in the world around us
and squeezing everything *out*
of the moment
not *in*.

It's only when the pace settles
and breaths deepen
that life can truly be absorbed.

We are always running out of time
and we know it
so start being here *now*
because we do not know
when that last grain of sand
will drop.

And you may miss the beauty of its moment
never miss the beauty of that moment.

YOUR WHOLE LIFE

Your whole life
you have cried
but did not drown

Your whole life
you have screamed
without a sound

Your whole life
you have bled
but did not die

Your whole life
you have toiled
without a why

Your whole life
you have broken
and repaired

Your whole life
you have given
you have shared

Your whole life
you have split
yourself in parts

Your whole life
was not yours
from the start

Your new life
is behind the next
closed door

Your new life
comes to even up
the score

Your new life
will see drama
disappear

Your new life
is devoid of
guilt and fear.

JOY

If something in your life is to be celebrated, celebrate it with all your might. You must live while the living is easy, you must seize the joy when it comes and not dim your light to match another's. It does not make you less human, it makes you more so. You can feel *all* things at once. Life is a cycle of ups and downs, always has been and always will be. There will never truly be peace on earth or a perfect time for your share of the good stuff. Honour your joy, someone else would give anything for it.

it's okay to feel weary sometimes

even when the weight

is that of your blessings

CHANGE

My friend
when change threatens
to whip the rug
from under your feet
or push you out
of your comfortable bubble
face it.

Look change
right in the eye
and let it know
that you have been changing
every day
since the day you were born
and you will do so
until the day you die

and you may not be quite ready
for this particular change *yet*
but you're not afraid.

Because you have done this many times.

Change got you where you are now

and look how far you've come.

SLIM

Yes you feel great when you're slim
because you feel more worthy somehow
in control
accepted
you fit in
and stand out
but for the *right* reasons
right?

You're slim, therefore, you're *okay*
regardless of the mess that's inside your mind
your body reflects peace
and that's important
right?

But you can have those feelings
without starving
without having to grind yourself to powder
every day.

Those feelings above
are not connected physically to your body shape
you attached them
society attached them
but you can *detach* them.

Extricate your worth
your peace
from your size
and stitch it to the inside of your soul
where it can live happily ever after.

Because your soul never changes
but your body *must*.

LOST

You haven't lost yourself my love.

It's about knowing
what to look for in the mirror
you see.

You won't find the old you in there
because you've *changed*
you've *evolved*
of *course* you have.

That isn't a failure
that's an achievement.

It's about finding the beauty in the new
instead of searching for the old.

You haven't lost her
you've grown
as you were supposed to
and you've done that beautifully
breaks and all.

There is much new beauty
you are simply not seeing.

Look again
with fresh eyes

there she is.

FLAWS

What if I told you
that in the act
of examining your body
for flaws
you will never be disappointed
(read that again).

What if I also told you
that if you stop looking
for flaws
you stop seeing them
(read that again too)

and after a while
they magically disappear.

Furthermore
no one else notices your flaws
because you're no longer pointing them out
or waiting for someone else
to do so.

What if I told you
that you can also decide
to see your flaws as anything *but*.

They are just parts of you
and they are perfectly loveable
if you *believe* them to be so.

So instead of changing
all that you dislike
why not spend your time
trying to like
all that you are.

WHEN WOMEN COME TOGETHER

When women come together
something magical happens
it's science, the mystical kind
an unstoppable force
to be reckoned with.

When women come together
they connect
on a deeper level
both spiritually and cellularly
souls nodding in alignment
I see you.

Put women together for long enough
and their cycles may sync
if that is not an example
of the wondrous, connective
majesty of womanhood
what is my friend, what is?

When women come together
an unseen wall is fashioned
built from the wisdom of the breaks
we have all endured
and the passion to scream louder
so that those beneath us can hear
and need not suffer the same.

When women come together
and tell their stories
the good and the bad
the power created
is a tsunami of strength
and intuition
washing us all on
to better things
a wave of magnificence
wisdom and sisterhood.

When women come together
we are, quite frankly
intimidating.

So watch out for those
who will keep us apart.

They are afraid
but we are not.

THE WISE OLD WOMAN

I once met a wise old woman
whose face spoke
of many hard years

She was eager to part me her wisdom
and her words surely moved me
to tears

Put it down
she said with great passion
That load which
you're carrying there
it was only supposed to be fleeting
but you've borne it for all
these long years

Which load I inquired with surprise
for my hands were as
empty as air

She placed her hand straight on my heart
It's the load that you have
right in here

Let it go now my child and be free
don't wear yourself thin
like I did

It's okay to drop it and leave it.
place it down now
go out and live.

THE CONCEPT OF AGE

Anti-ageing as a concept is like trying to rewind the sunset every morning. It cannot be done. You are ageing, every minute of every day. There is no way to reverse that, it is the fundamental journey of life. Why not get used to that now and start to enjoy the process, instead of dreading it and fighting. Believe me, there is much beauty you are missing. The sunrise may be gone today but the sunset is just as beautiful, if not more so. And so are you. So are you.

I HAVE LAUGHED

I have laughed
oh how I have laughed.

I have laughed so hard
with so many wonderful people
that I now wear the marks.

Mother Nature has engraved me as one
who laughed whenever she could.

I wear the tattoo of the joyful
and that makes me swell with pride.

How can I hate upon these lines
when I remember the nights
the music, the dancing, the fun
the tears of laughter
and the blindingly joyful light.

Give me a mark for every night
I felt alive
and I will show them to the world
with pride.

I have laughed
oh how I have laughed.

I hope you have laughed too my friend.
And if you have not
start now

you've some joyous catching up to do.

MEN DON'T AGE BETTER

Men don't age better than women
men age without fear
without worry, without judgement.

Men age secure in the knowledge
that it's as it should be
and the fight is not theirs to take on.

Men age without prying eyes looking for lines
looking for grey hairs or spare fat
men just *age*
freedom looks good on them
does it not?

Women age with the eyes of the world upon them
lest they be considered to have let themselves *go*
or lost a battle in the war.

Women age with the rules and restrictions
of dressing correctly for 'their age'
employing new make-up techniques
to hide drooping eyelids
and steer attention away from the wrinkles.

Women age with the burden of beauty
and the expectations of society
wearing them down
and creating even more pressure than before
making it harder to look 'well'.

Men don't age better than women
they age without guilt for 'losing their looks'
and that is worth a million new lotions, potions
or pills promising youth.

Let's try it and see
if freedom looks good on us all.

INVISIBLE

It's not that you become invisible with age. It's that you no longer attract the **wrong** attention. Your energy is so very finely tuned to its own unique frequency that you move around in safety and peace. You vibrate with strength, dignity and wisdom, and that does not invite strangers, only friends you haven't yet met. You have earned yourself this right to feel invincible, not invisible. Never *invisible*. Enjoy the space you have built for yourself, my friend, and honour its boundaries the way they deserve to be honoured. Invincible, never invisible . . .

SO OLD

You're so old
they say
and I laugh
with a deep roar
rising up from my very core
because how could that phrase
ever be anything
but *magnificent?*

She let herself go
they cry
and I smile
with every tooth in my head
because Mother Nature and I know
what a miraculous act
letting go
truly is.

You've changed
they say
and I am at once
completely fulfilled
and at peace
with my life's purpose
because if I did not come here
to grow
then what was it all for?

THE EMPTY NEST

My nest is as it should be now
empty

Tidy, ordered
calm.

My babies have grown, beautifully
and flown.
Just the way I taught them to.

And my heart is full of pride, and love
still so full of love.

But oh there is an ache there
a throb, a pang.
I have given of myself in a way
that only a mother can
so consuming is that gift
there is scarce room
for much else to thrive.

So what now?

My empty nest feels hollow
the echo of my own breath
rings in my ears.

My worries have not flown
with the fledglings
they linger still
but now without the comfort
of a slumbering head
on a pillow upstairs.

My imagination tells the tales
I don't want to see
and my spare time
once so coveted
is now my enemy.

My nest is as it should be now
empty.

But I will not be empty, little one.

I will fly, just like you
find my new place in this story.

Play music, bring friends
make noise and laughter
and fill the house with life
so that when you come home
you see nothing to worry about here
for that may clip
your beautiful wings.

And you will remember
how nurturing your nest once was
and you will crave the feeling of it
just once in a while.

This nest will never close
and nor will I let it lose its love.

Fly, my loves, fly
but remember the way back home.

TEACH

Don't teach your children to win. Teach them how to lose, without letting it affect their self-esteem. Teach them how to help others lose well too. Let them be the kid that waits behind to run with someone who can't. That kid will forge through life, mending, bonding, inspiring, creating, yet maybe never winning a race. That kid will have control of their own self-worth and not put it in the hands of so many variables. That kid will have access to the peace that not requiring outside validation brings. What a gift to one so young. Don't teach your children to win my friend, teach them to lose. That's the hardest lesson to learn.

LIFE BEGINS

Life doesn't begin at 40
or at the end of your comfort zone.

Life begins the day you decide
that it does.

The day you realise
that each day you open your eyes
and take a breath
is another day you have been gifted
on this planet

The day you realise
not everyone is so blessed
with that gift
as you are right now.

How so many others did not wake up
to see this new day
no matter how rainy
or stressful
that day may be.

The day you look around and realise
that beauty and joy can be found
in
every
single
moment.

If you look.

That's when your life truly begins
and wow, does it begin.

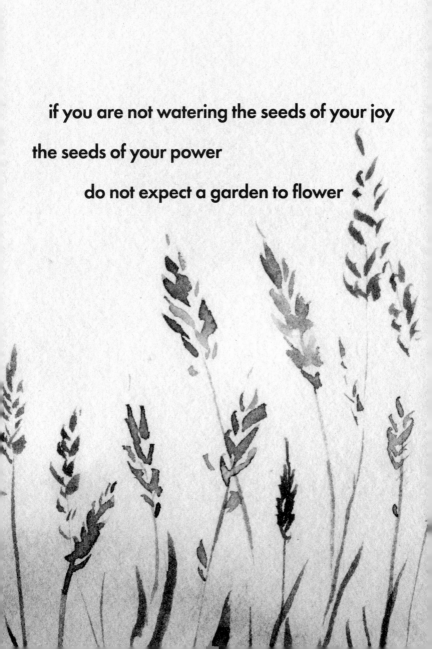

if you are not watering the seeds of your joy

the seeds of your power

do not expect a garden to flower

YOUNGER

Don't tell me I look young
for my age
or that I do not display
the passing of my years
for that is not something
I strive to win.

Tell me I look strong
or wise
tell me I have a great smile
or I light up a room
tell me I am infectiously positive
or comfortingly real.

Tell me I am thought-provoking
energy-replenishing
or magic-making.

Tell me nothing, perhaps
just sit with me
and let our souls talk
but do not fill the empty silence
with compliments that are not so.

It is no feat to look young for our age.

It is no achievement
to have battled the years and won

the achievement actually comes
from not caring
about that
very much
at all.

PRECIOUS

This world wants you to spend your precious time and money fighting the ageing process and desperately trying not to take up too much space, when you could be spending both on adventures, new experiences and spiritual journeys. All of which you will share with your loved ones, inspiring generations to come. Don't be fooled, beautiful one, you are not here to preserve, to mummify yourself in life, you are here to live. It's your stories, your advice and your love which will last long after your death. Your body has a shelf life but your soul does not. Wear your body out, in the most beautiful ways, it was always meant to be so.

LET ME AGE

Let me age
for I have earned
a home
in skin too loose

Let me age
for I have toiled
for the peace
which follows the noose

Let me age
for I have come
to embrace the lines
and all they are

Let me age
for I have worked
to see such beauty
in my scars

Let me age
for don't you see
nature wanted this
to be

Let me age
for with that act
comes the art of
being free.

WHEN WE'RE OLDER

When we're older let's meet every Sunday at four
in that cute little café we love
let's laugh at our foibles, our mishaps and then
release our mistakes to above

We can share a new wrinkle, a hair that's turned grey
and marvel at how we have grown
we can both reminisce on the lives that we've led
and be grateful for each day we've known

When we're older let's meet by that tree in the park
the one where the blossom grows yearly
we can share what we have and toast with a drink
remembering those we loved dearly

We will not give a thought to the youth we have lost
for we see so much worth in the change
we won't feel the rush of a fast-ticking clock
for we know time is ours to arrange

When we're older, let's meet every Sunday at four
in that cute little café we love
Let's be wowed by how we have weathered this life
let's release our regrets to‾above.

THE COLOUR IN AGE

The freedom and wisdom
that growing older brings
allows you
urges you in fact
to seek out your most beautiful shades
which were hidden for so long.

To let that spectrum shine through
resplendent, honest and true.

Your true colours.

The freedom and wisdom
that growing older brings
is an almost unstoppable force
pushing your real self out of hiding
pulling her into the spotlight
stripping her of all unnecessary care
and *abandoning* her
to the glory of acceptance.

The freedom and wisdom
that growing older brings
allows you
urges you in fact
to reveal
the very shades of you
the world painted black.

Channel your inner rainbow ladies
it's truly time.

THE CONTENTED CRONE

I've always wanted, very much
to be *that woman*.

The old one
with the hair like silver
that seems to radiate
her very own source of cosmic light.

The one with the knowing smile
that hints at humour ever present
and a life that's been full
of joy and belly laughter.

The woman with the deep lines
in her weathered skin
lines etched out by both
adventure and growth.

I imagined how I'd float
rather than walk
despite ageing bones
because I no longer bear
the weight of the world
on my shoulders.

And I would marvel at days
full to the brim
of simply *being*
and *noticing*
the silent beauty
of the world
that was always around me.

I would not tolerate thoughts of guilt
because by then I would have learned
that resting is *doing*
and is very important indeed.

There I would be reading
gardening
eating delicious food I had grown myself
and passing my little nuggets of wisdom down
to anyone with hearing ears
and inquisitive eyes.

The contented crone.

The final phase in the journey
of womanity.

No chasing youth for me
I will be languishing
loudly
in the joy of my age
amazed at my luck
for having got so far.

I've always wanted
very much
to be *that woman*.

Join me
if you like.

ASK ME MY AGE

Ask me my age
I won't think you rude
for the years are not
dragging me down
I have toiled in the depths
of the gold-mine of life
and I'm happy to share
what I've found

Ask me my age
I'll show you the lines
each one shows a
laugh or a frown
I won't worry or fret
they're hiding my light
for the soul is a ship
that won't drown

Ask me my age
don't offer your salve
that I look so much
younger to you
when you've come as far
as the journey I've made
you don't care

if you're battered
and bruised.

ACKNOWLEDGEMENTS

Thank you for buying this book, or if someone has gifted it to you, remember each time you open the pages, how very valued you are. I would love to see you on my social media accounts where we daily remind each other, that life is not always easy, but it's always for the *living*.

*'Every day is a new twist and a new turn
but nothing, **nothing** lasts forever.'*

*'Shine bright little fighter,
this dark world needs your glow.'*

If you have been affected by any of the topics raised in *Life*, you may find it helpful to talk to your partner, a relative, friend or reach out to one of the services below. You do not have to be in a crisis to call, you might just need a listening ear or to find help for a friend in need.

Age UK
Information and advice for people over 50.
www.ageuk.org.uk

Samaritans
Round the clock support for anyone who needs to talk.
www.samaritans.org

Mind
Dedicated to better mental health, Mind provides details
of resources and support in your area.
www.mind.org.uk

Beat Eating Disorders
Treatment information, advice and support for anyone
struggling with or caring for someone with an eating disorder.
www.beateatingdisorders.org.uk

Relate
For help with all kinds of relationships, whether they are
past, present or future, problematic or perfect.
www.relate.org.uk

SAMH
For support and information in Scotland, SAMH
also offers free, safe and confidential access to qualified
mental health professionals online.
www.samh.org.uk

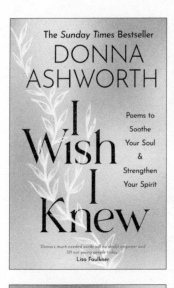

The *Sunday Times* Bestseller

DONNA ASHWORTH

I Wish I Knew

Poems to Soothe Your Soul & Strengthen Your Spirit

Donna's much-needed words will no doubt empower and lift our young people today.
Lisa Faulkner

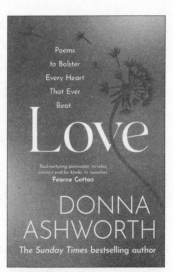

Poems to Bolster Every Heart That Ever Beat

Love

Soul-nurturing permission to relax, connect and be kinder to ourselves
Fearne Cotton

DONNA ASHWORTH

The *Sunday Times* bestselling author

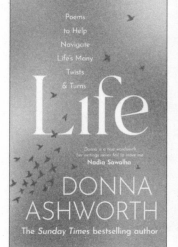

Poems to Help Navigate Life's Many Twists & Turns

Life

Donna is a true wordsmith, her writings never fail to move me
Nadia Sawalha

DONNA ASHWORTH

The *Sunday Times* bestselling author

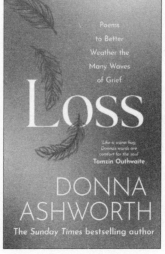

Poems to Better Weather the Many Waves of Grief

Loss

Like a warm hug, Donna's words are comfort for the soul
Tamzin Outhwaite

DONNA ASHWORTH

The *Sunday Times* bestselling author

Donna Ashworth is a *Sunday Times* bestselling author and a lover of words who lives happily in the hills of Scotland with her husband, two sons, and Brian and Dave (the dogs). Donna started her social media accounts in 2018 and is astounded daily by the international reach her words have garnered.

"My dream was to connect with women all over the world, so we could look at each other and say *I see you, this is hard* and just generally agree that imperfection is to be celebrated not feared."

When she is not writing, Donna loves to eat, be merry and laugh; believing these to be the best medicines life can offer.

Instagram @DonnaAshworthWords
TikTok @DonnaAshworthWordy
facebook.com/ladiespassiton
www.donnaashworth.com